A Glass **Half Empty?** ...or **Half Full?**

A Children's Book for Grown Ups

A Glass **Half Empty?** ...or **Half Full?**

A Children's Book for Grown Ups

By Dan Schuck

Glass Half Question
2018

First Printing: 2018

ISBN: 978-1-54393-030-6

Glass Half Question
7190 W Sunset Blvd #102
Los Angeles, CA 90046

www.glasshalfquestion.com

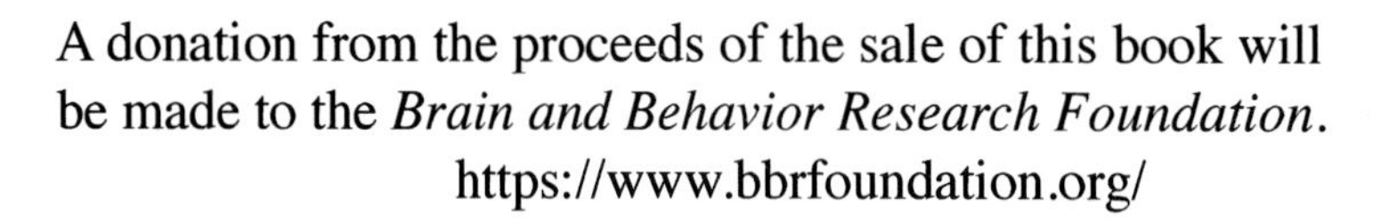
A donation from the proceeds of the sale of this book will be made to the *Brain and Behavior Research Foundation*.
https://www.bbrfoundation.org/

For Jill,

My soulmate, my inamorata, my teacher, and my inspiration.

I will *Love* You Forever.

Valentine's Day, 2018

You've heard **The Question** before.

Some form of it exists in every language across the globe, and its origins are as ancient as the human spirit.

Is your Glass...

It’s supposed to mean...

Are you...

A Pessimist?

A SOURPUSS?

A Worry Wart?

Gloomy?

a killjoy?

A Cynic?

a Wet Blanket?

A Misanthrope?

THE PROPHET
OF DOOM?

...or

An Optimist?

A POSITIVE THINKER?

Cheerful?

ENTHUSIASTIC?

hopeful?

Confident?

Happy?

It's also supposed to mean…

Are you…

A Realist?

Down to Earth?

logical?

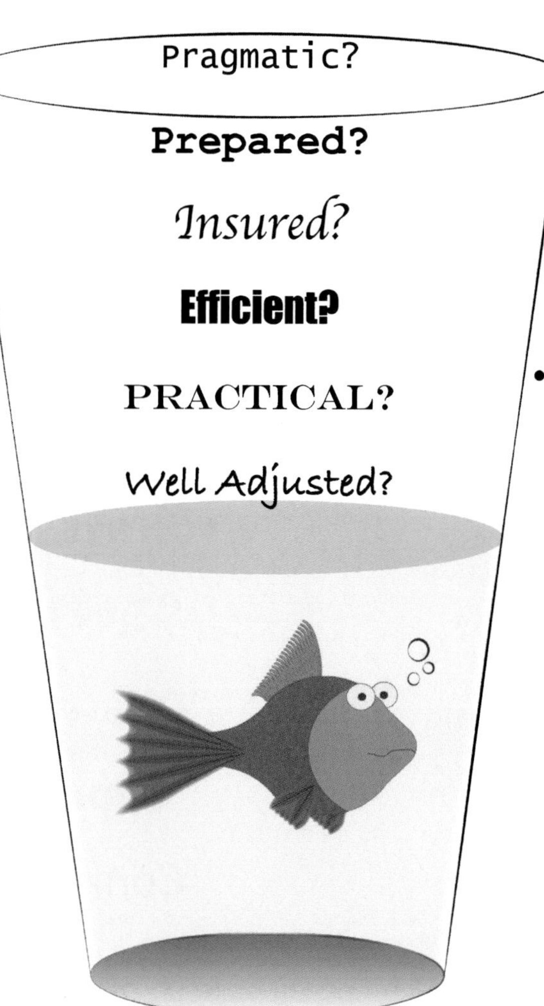

…or

An Idealist?

a Dreamer?

SANGUINE?

UNREALISTIC?

Confused?

A Pollyanna?

Delusional?

But there are more important lessons that we can learn from

The Question.

or basically, your Life...

...then we all know our Glass is...

rarely,

truly,

exactly,

Half Empty

...or

Half Full.

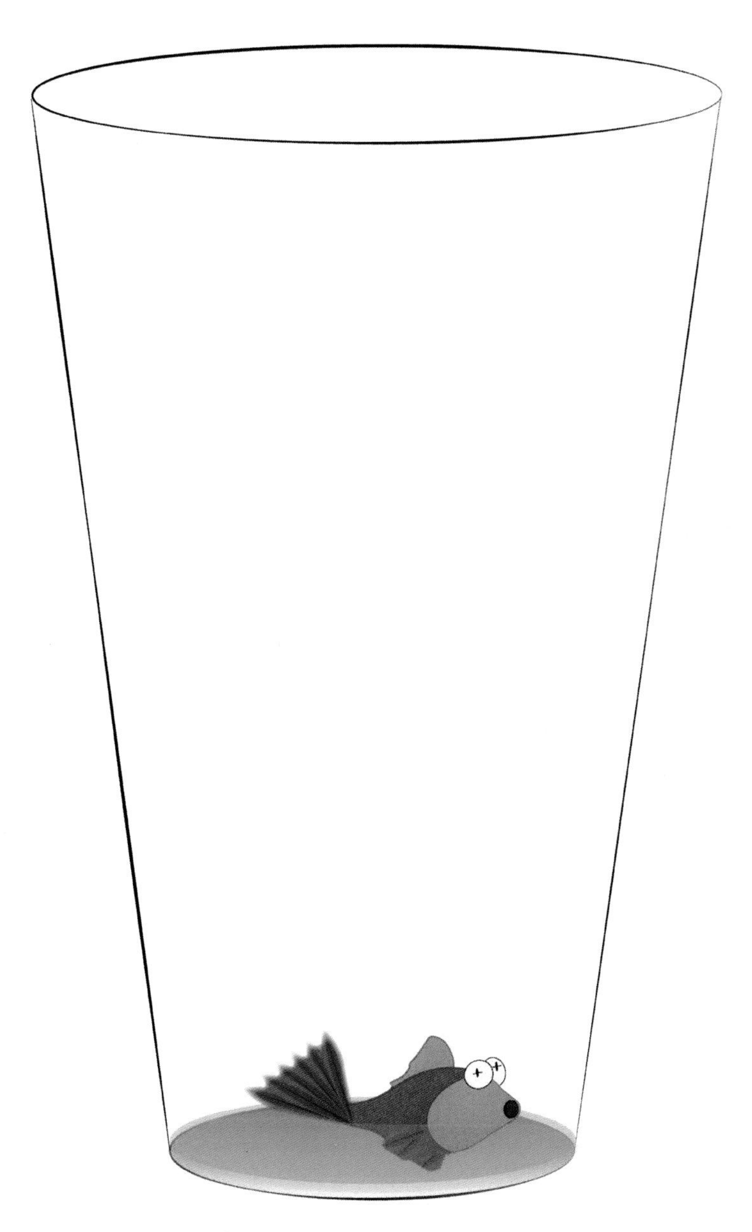

Too little is clearly not good.

But too much can create different kinds of challenges.

Of course, what you put into your Glass matters a lot!

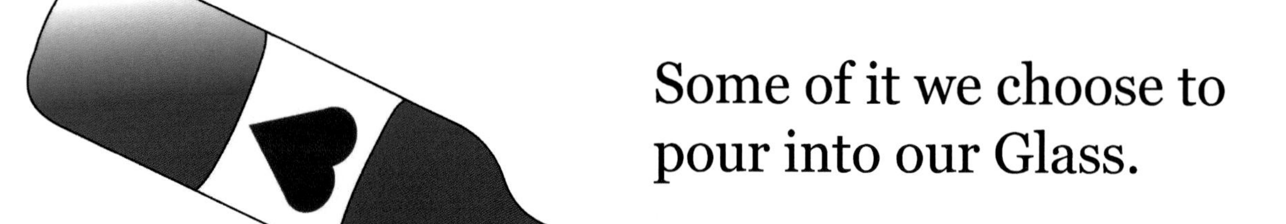

Some of it we choose to pour into our Glass.

Hobbies

Community Involvement

Music

School Participation

Exercise

Extracurricular Activites

SPORTS

Reading

Church

Entertainment

Gag Gifts

ICE CREAM

Meditation

FINE WINE

Binge Watching

Being “Productive” on the Internet

SHOPPING

Some of it we do NOT choose, but it gets poured into our Glass anyway.

DISEASE

The Neighbors' Music

Exhaustion

POVERTY

bug Bites

Boredom

Dirty Diapers

GRIEF

Teenagers with Drivers Licenses

Addiction

BULLYING

Income Tax

Injuries

PHOBIAS

Disabilities

ARREST RECORDS

SUBWAY SMELLS

Nagging

The parts we don’t choose ourselves, often comes from others...

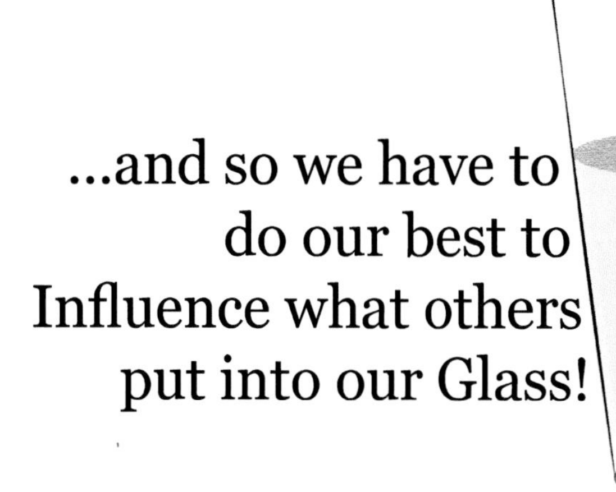

...and so we have to do our best to Influence what others put into our Glass!

Whatever the mix, we each have to drink from our own Glass.

Whatever the mix, it's always changing.

What's actually
in the Glass
is never
exactly the same
from day to day.

Some guard what's in their Glass unnecessarily...

And some drink from their Glass
faster than they can refill it.

Although we don't get complete control over everything that gets put into our Glass....

...we do control what we put into each other's Glasses.

Filling each others' Glasses

is part of how we help

Replenish our own Glass.

Think

about it as

INVESTING

in another's

Glass.

The most powerful INVESTMENTS we can make are

Love and **HATRED**....

When we put these into another's Glass,

they pay back large dividends.

Hint: Choose *Love*...

You don't want **HATRED** dividends paying out to your Glass!

Most of us have
CRACKS in our Glass....

...and there is some
threat that we may lose
some of what we have.

This is called...

Risk

Danger

A GAMBLE

Personal Exposure

UNCERTAINTY

The Unforeseen

Peril

a Liability

Debt

What's Lurking
Around The Corner

Obligation

Being an Adult

You can't avoid it.

Everyone has Risk.

And ignoring your Risk can lead to a very empty Glass.

A very Full Glass has a lot more Risk.

Ever spill from a very Full Glass?

How about from a **Half Empty/Half Full** Glass?

And it's not fair that some have more Risk than others.

Life and Glasses are fragile and unique.
No two are alike.

But if you become consumed with managing your Risk...

...you might miss out on enjoying a drink from your Glass.

And what's the point of that?

Remember, whether you put it there,
or someone else puts it there...

...your Glass

is

always

being

refilled.

And what about this space above the water line in your Glass?

What is that called?

This is called...

Opportunity

Hope

POTENTIAL

Your Big Shot

Scope

BEING OPEN TO CHANGE

Prayer

Faith

a First Date

Time and Space

THE TRUST OF YOUR FRIENDS AND FAMILY

The Winning Numbers!

Opportunity is the space we need to
Replenish our Glass.

It might even be
misleading to call
that space “empty.”

It’s really more like:
“filled with Opportunity!”

It is so important to have Opportunity in your Glass that sometimes you have to Make Space for it.

This can beanything from:

GETTING RID OF EXCESS BAGGAGE

to

MAKING SACRIFICES,

...and usually some of both.

But let’s be real: Too much “Opportunity…”

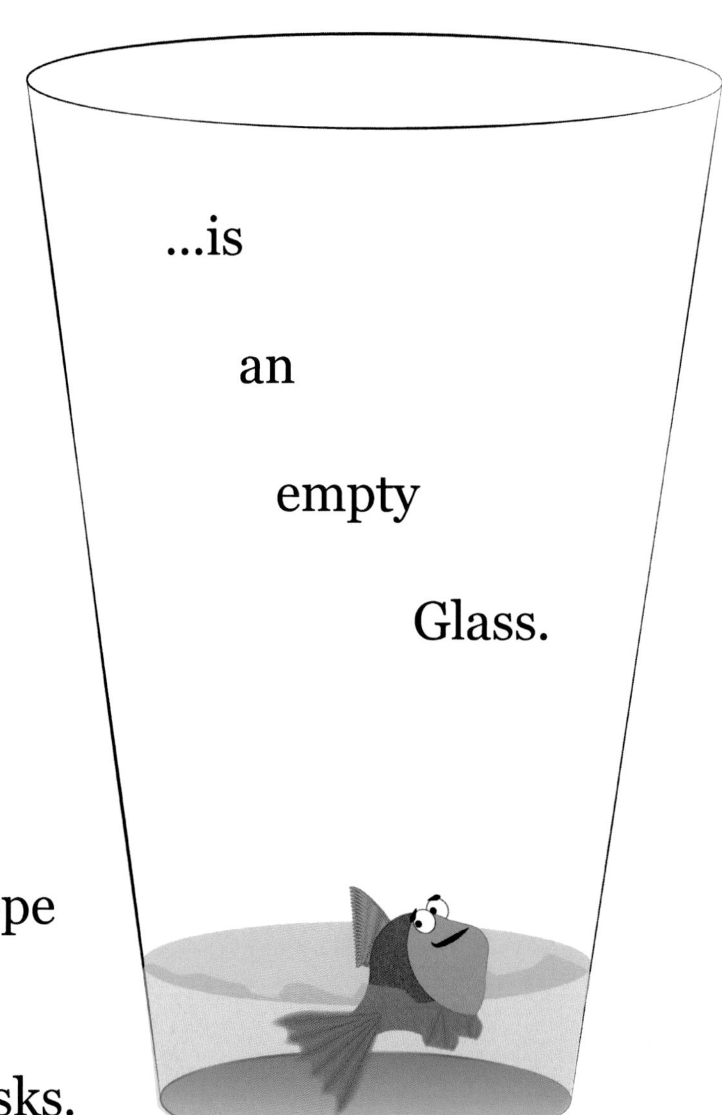

…is

an

empty

Glass.

Living in
denial and false hope
is just as bad
as ignoring your Risks.

We each have to use our own judgement about finding a balance...

...between appreciating the Opportunity in our Glass...

...and appreciating that which we already have in our Glass.

Appreciate your Opportunity.
Influence what gets poured into your Glass.
?
Invest in other's Glasses.
Manage your Risk.
Drink,
Refill,
Repeat.
Over Flow Drain
...are you dizzy yet?

It's Life ... and it's complicated!

...try keeping your focus on the horizon.

If you'll just stay focused on the Balance in your Glass...

...you'll be just fine.

So, do you know
the answer to
The Question
now?

Is your Glass...

NEITHER!
Both!
Yes.
NO.
Ask me again tomorrow...
Maybe!!
Why thank you for asking!